WORLD WINDOWS

Thomas Edison

HEINLE
CENGAGE Learning™

Y|S|G
A YBM COMPANY
Young & Son
Global, Inc.

What do you think is the most important invention in history?

1879 | **light bulb**
Thomas Edison

| 1870 | 1880 | 1890 |

1876 | **telephone**
Alexander Graham Bell

1891 | **movie camera**
Thomas Edison

Witnesses:

1903   **airplane**
Wright Brothers

1900   1910

Contents

inventors

inventions

experiment

phonograph

light bulb

movie camera

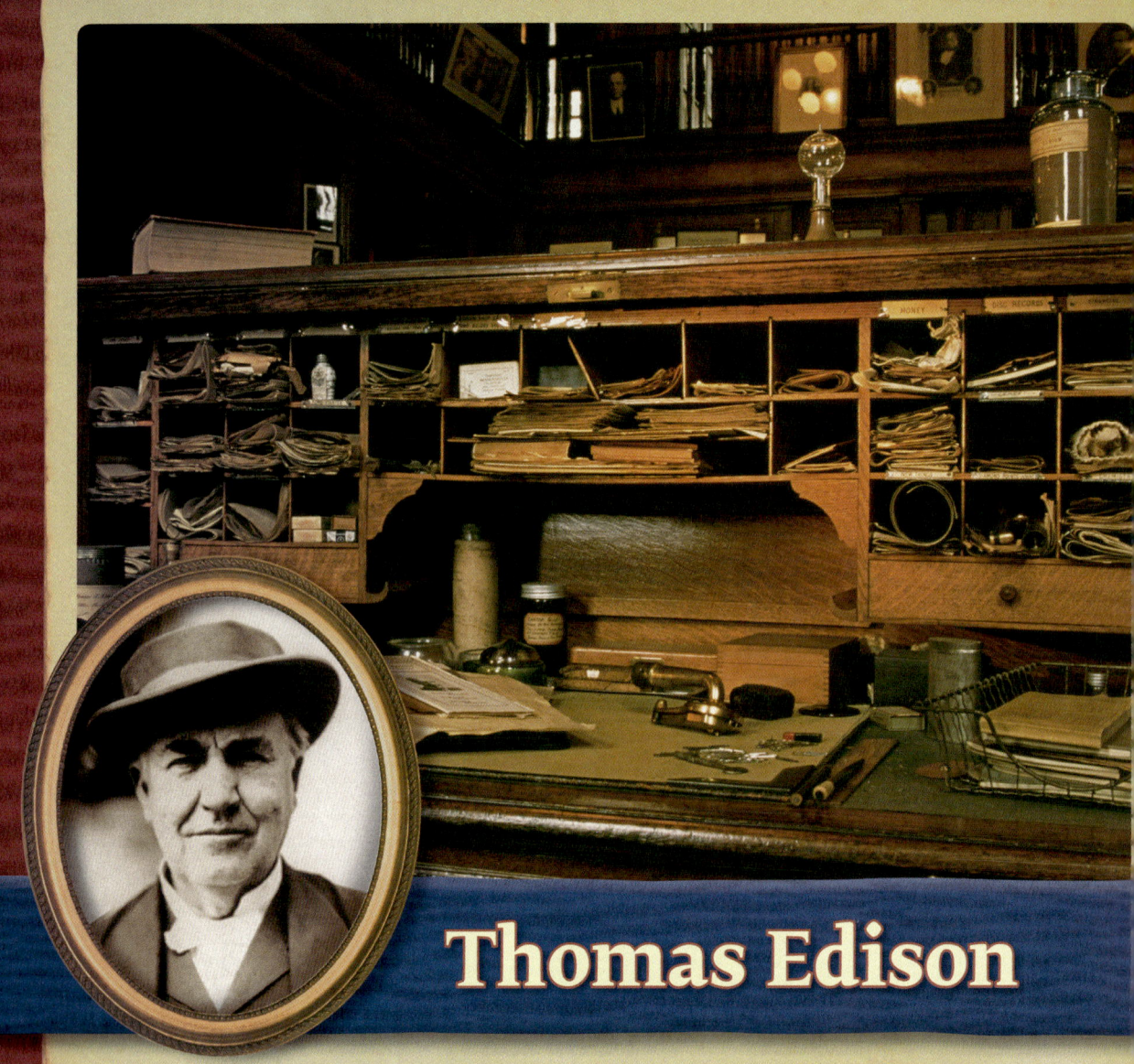

Thomas Edison

Thomas Edison was an inventor.
He invented more than 1,000 things over his lifetime.
We still use many of his inventions in our everyday lives.

Thomas Edison's birthplace

1847 ～ His Birth

Thomas Edison was born in 1847 in the state of Ohio, in the United States of America.

Young Thomas was always curious about how things worked.

1859 ～ His Childhood

He loved doing experiments.
He started selling newspapers and
candy from the age of 12.
He used the money to do experiments.

1876 ~ His Laboratory

In 1876, Thomas Edison moved to Menlo Park, New Jersey.
He built a laboratory and used it for some of his greatest inventions.

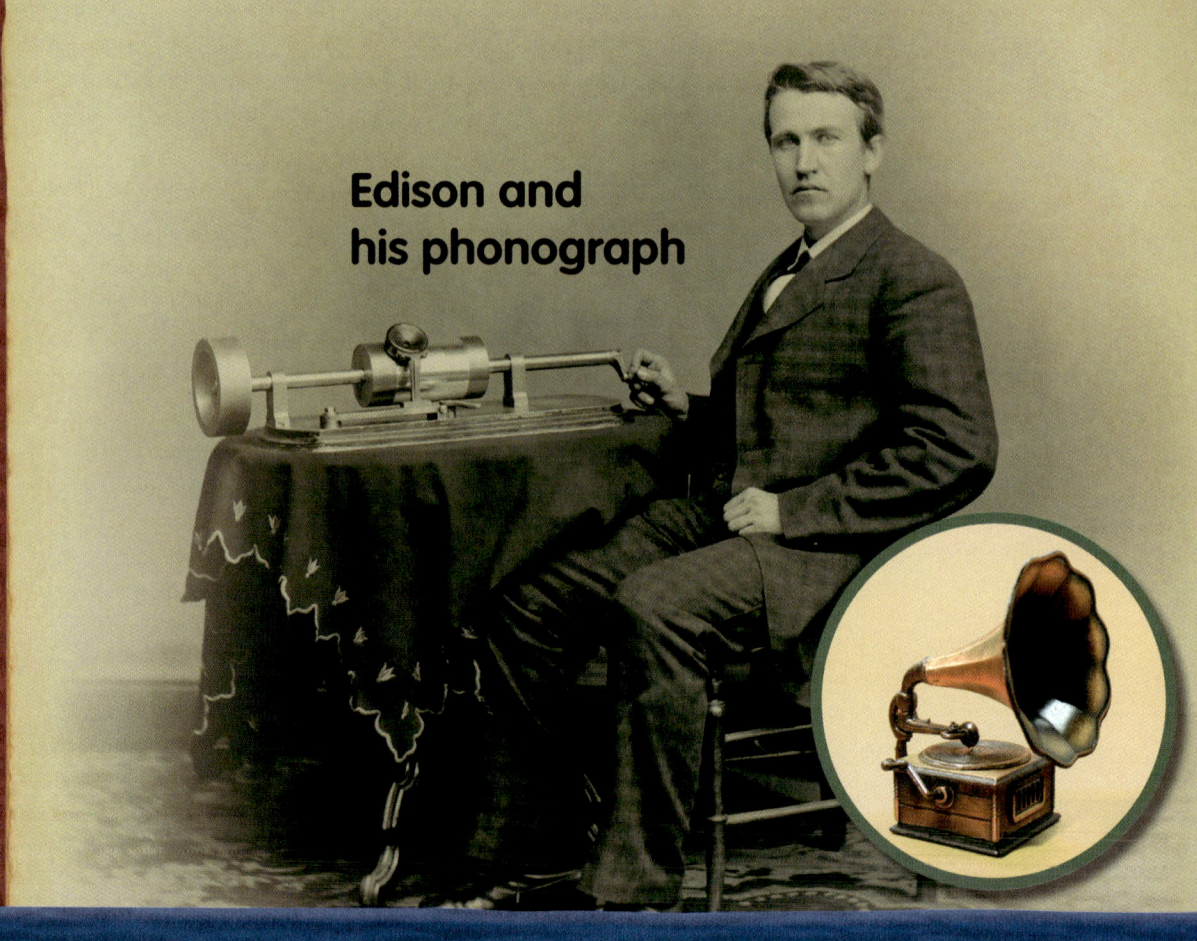

Edison and his phonograph

1877 〜 Phonograph

He invented the phonograph in 1877. The phonograph recorded sound and played it back.

People started to record music after his invention.

Edison's light bulb

1879 ～ Electric Light Bulb

One of his most important inventions was the electric light bulb.

He tried and failed many times, but he finally made the light bulb work in 1879. Now, people everywhere use light bulbs.

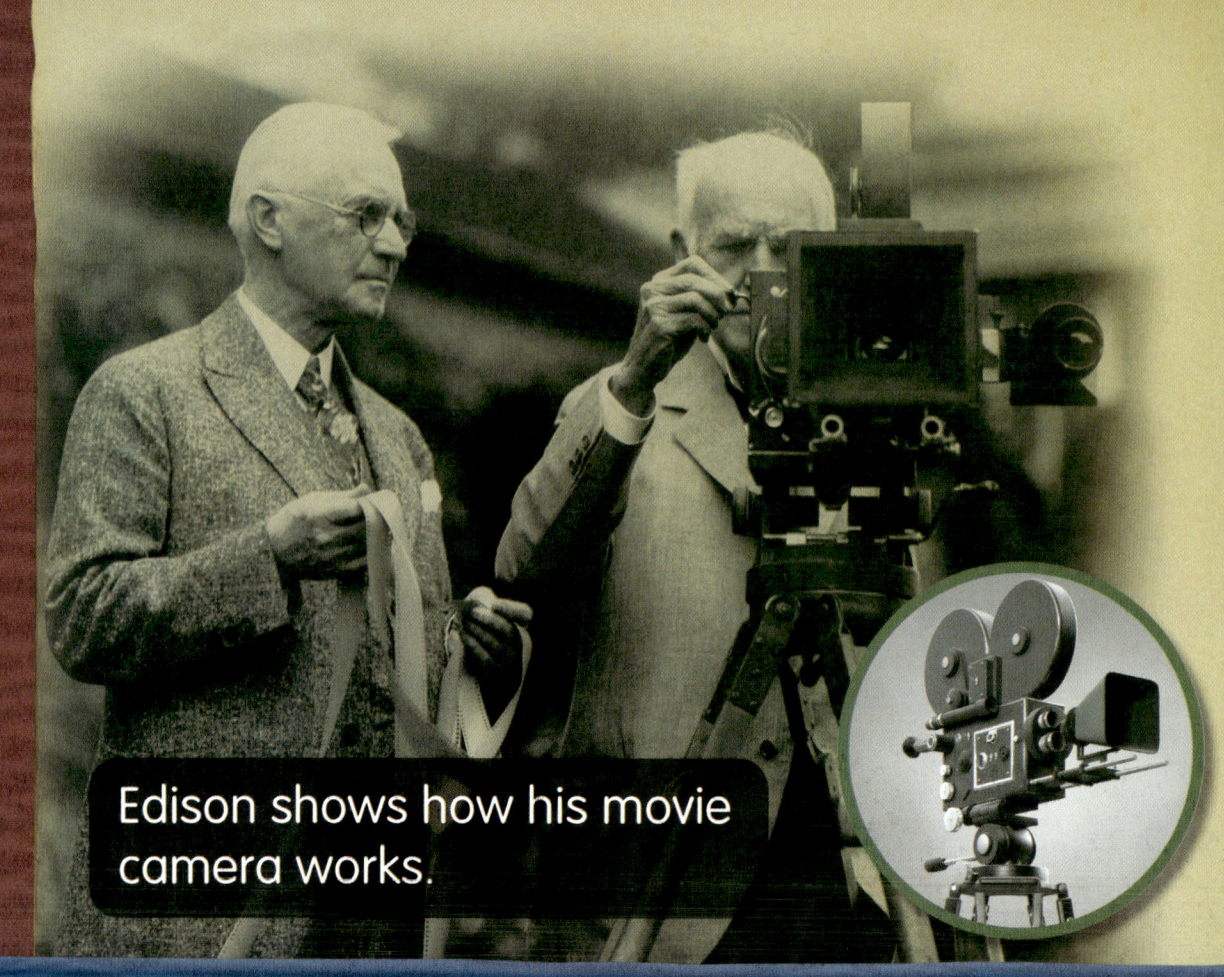

Edison shows how his movie camera works.

1891 〜 Movie Camera

In 1891, Edison invented an early type of movie camera.

It showed a movie through a small hole. Because of his invention, people could watch movies.

Thomas Edison's life

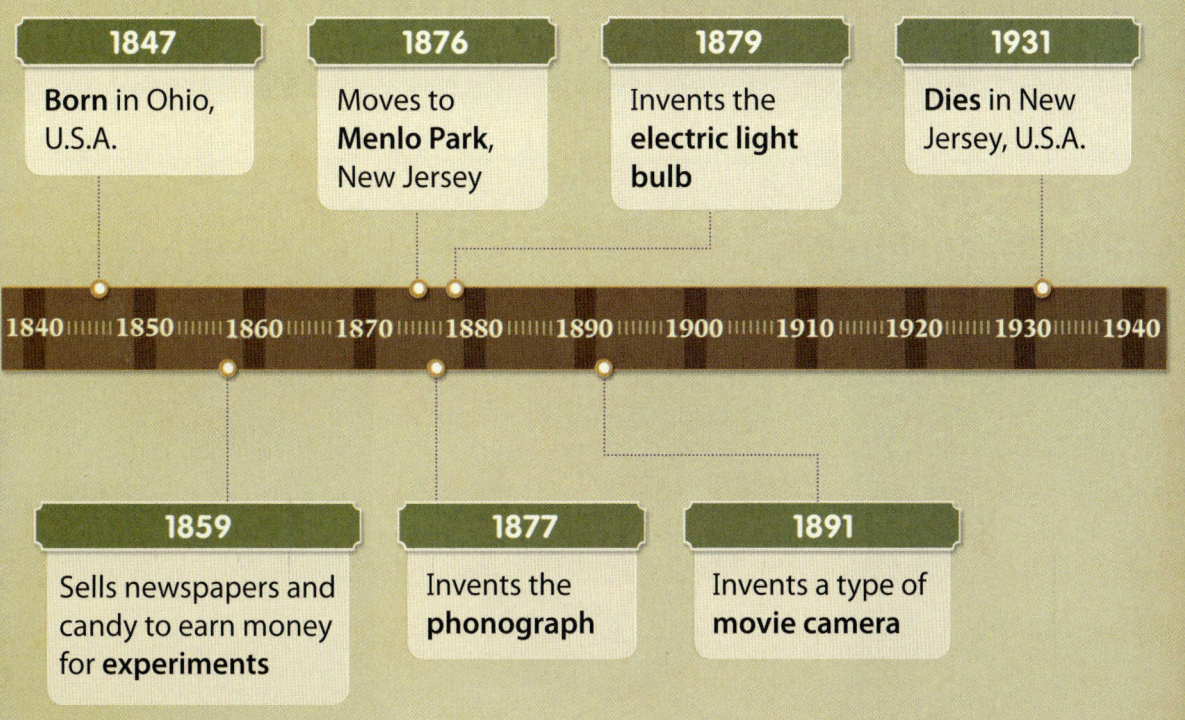

1847
Born in Ohio, U.S.A.

1876
Moves to **Menlo Park,** New Jersey

1879
Invents the **electric light bulb**

1931
Dies in New Jersey, U.S.A.

1840 1850 1860 1870 1880 1890 1900 1910 1920 1930 1940

1859
Sells newspapers and candy to earn money for **experiments**

1877
Invents the **phonograph**

1891
Invents a type of **movie camera**

1931 ～ His Death

Thomas Edison continued inventing until he died in 1931.
He will always be remembered as one of the greatest inventors of all time.

What did Thomas Edison invent?

Read a Timeline

A **timeline** shows important events in the order in which they happened. A timeline is read from left to right.

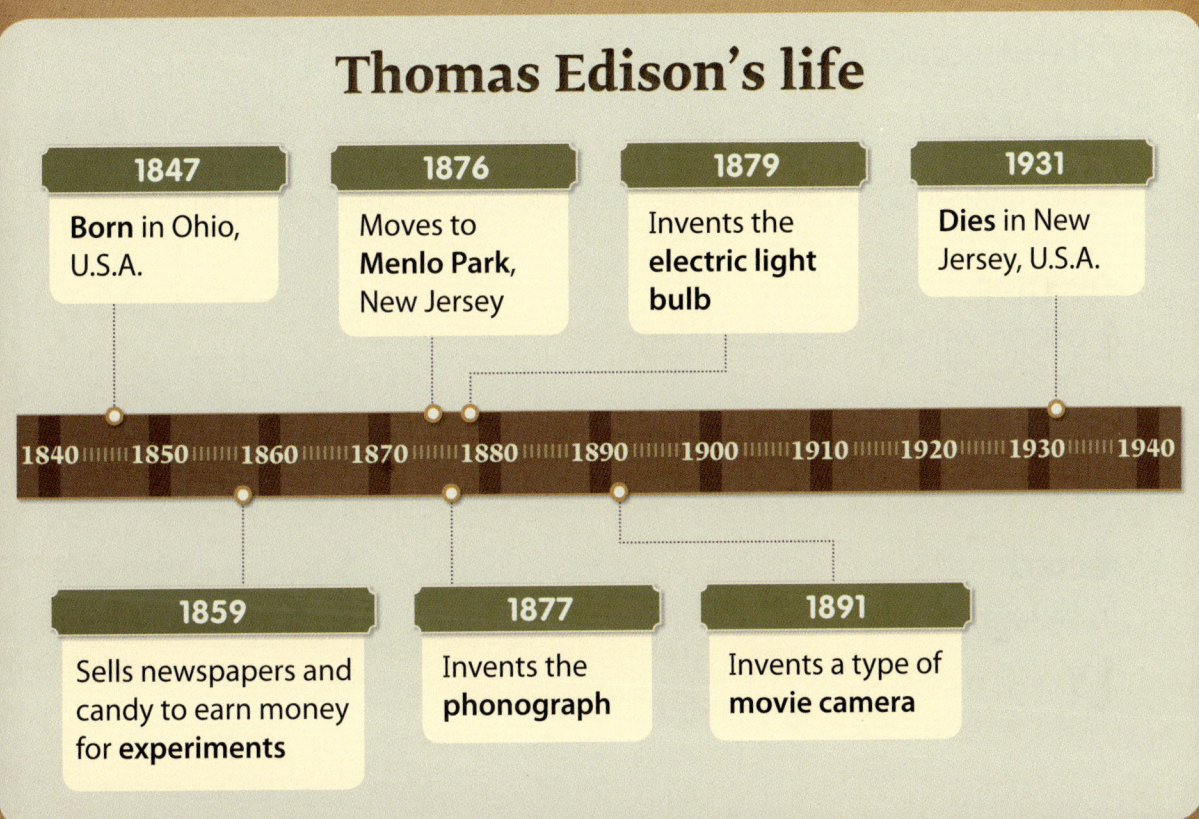

Thomas Edison's life

1847	1876	1879	1931
Born in Ohio, U.S.A.	Moves to **Menlo Park, New Jersey**	Invents the **electric light bulb**	**Dies** in New Jersey, U.S.A.

1840 | 1850 | 1860 | 1870 | 1880 | 1890 | 1900 | 1910 | 1920 | 1930 | 1940

1859	1877	1891
Sells newspapers and candy to earn money for **experiments**	Invents the **phonograph**	Invents a type of **movie camera**

1. What did Thomas Edison invent in 1877?

2. What happened in 1891?

3. When did Thomas Edison die?

Glossary

curious
Wanting to know or learn about something

experiment
A scientific test to find out what happens to someone or something

fail
To be unsuccessful when you try to do something

invention
A machine, tool, or system that someone has made for the first time

inventor
A person who creates new things

laboratory
A place designed for scientific experiments

record
To store sounds or moving pictures so that they can be heard or seen later

Index